Leafy Seadragons

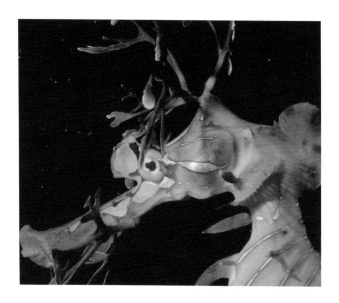

words by Robyn Opie
photographs by David Muirhead

This is a sea dragon.

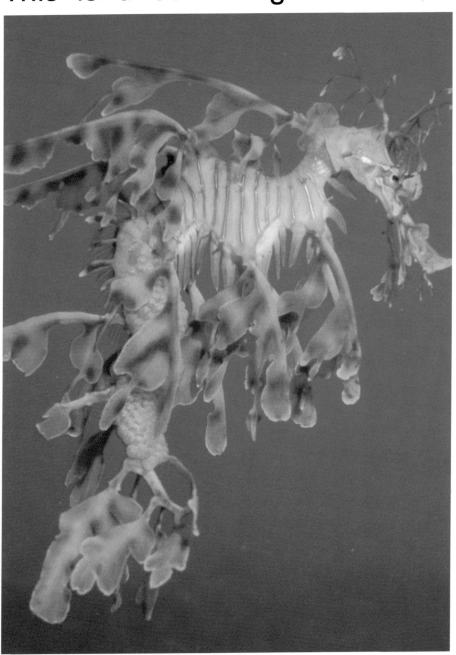

Sea dragons are like sea horses.

There are two kinds
of sea dragons.
This is a weedy sea dragon.

This is a leafy sea dragon.

Leafy sea dragons look
like seaweed.
This is how they hide.

Leafy sea dragons eat tiny sea animals.

They eat tiny fish eggs too.

Female leafy sea dragons
lay eggs.

But male leafy sea dragons
look after the eggs.

Sea dragons live in reefs and seaweed.

Pollution is killing reefs and seaweed.

We make the pollution.

We must keep the sea clean.

We must help the
sea dragons to live.